NEW YORKERS

SHORT STORIES

What makes one city different from another city? Is it the buildings, the weather, the people? It is the people who make a city, and to know a city, you must know its people. You must know what makes them laugh and cry, know the small details of their everyday lives.

What kind of people lived in New York at the beginning of the twentieth century? Are New Yorkers different now from a hundred years ago? Cities grow bigger with the years, new buildings are put up and old buildings are pulled down, horses are replaced by cars and buses, fashions change. But people do not change. The New Yorkers in these stories are very different from each other, but the hopes of a tramp are as important as the hopes of a lawyer; the love of a waitress is as exciting as the love of an actress. And we see that people's hopes and fears and dreams do not change with the years.

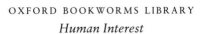

OXFORD BOOKWORMS LIBRARY

Human Interest

New Yorkers

SHORT STORIES

Stage 2 (700 headwords)

Series Editor: Jennifer Bassett
Founder Editor: Tricia Hedge
Activities Editors: Jennifer Bassett and Alison Baxter

O. HENRY

New Yorkers

SHORT STORIES

Retold by
Diane Mowat

OXFORD UNIVERSITY PRESS

OXFORD

UNIVERSITY PRESS

Great Clarendon Street, Oxford OX2 6DP

Oxford University Press is a department of the University of Oxford.
It furthers the University's objective of excellence in research, scholarship,
and education by publishing worldwide in

Oxford New York

Auckland Cape Town Dar es Salaam Hong Kong Karachi
Kuala Lumpur Madrid Melbourne Mexico City Nairobi
New Delhi Shanghai Taipei Toronto

With offices in

Argentina Austria Brazil Chile Czech Republic France Greece
Guatemala Hungary Italy Japan Poland Portugal Singapore
South Korea Switzerland Thailand Turkey Ukraine Vietnam

Any websites referred to in this publication are in the public domain and
their addresses are provided by Oxford University Press for information only.
Oxford University Press disclaims any responsibility for the content

ISBN 978 0 19 479067 3

A complete recording of this Bookworms edition of
New Yorkers is available on audio CD ISBN 978 0 19 478990 5

Printed in China

Illustrated by: Susan Scott

Word count (main text): 5895 words

For more information on the Oxford Bookworms Library,
visit www.oup.com/bookworms

CONTENTS

INTRODUCTION   i

The Christmas Presents   1
Soapy's Choice   9
A Walk in Amnesia   17
Tildy's Moment   27
The Memento   33

GLOSSARY   40
ACTIVITIES: Before Reading   43
ACTIVITIES: While Reading   44
ACTIVITIES: After Reading   46
ABOUT THE AUTHOR   52
ABOUT THE BOOKWORMS LIBRARY   53

The Christmas Presents

One dollar and eighty-seven cents. That was all. Every day, when she went to the shops, she spent very little money. She bought the cheapest meat, the cheapest vegetables. And when she was tired, she still walked round and round the shops to find the cheapest food. She saved every cent possible.

Della counted the money again. There was no mistake. One dollar and eighty-seven cents. That was all. And the next day was Christmas.

She couldn't do anything about it. She could only sit down and cry. So she sat there, in the poor little room, and she cried.

Della lived in this poor little room, in New York, with her husband, James Dillingham Young. They also had a bedroom, and a kitchen and a bathroom – all poor little rooms. James Dillingham Young was lucky, because he had a job, but it was not a good job. These rooms took most of his money. Della tried to find work, but times were bad, and there was no work for her. But when Mr James Dillingham Young came home to his rooms, Mrs James Dillingham Young called him 'Jim' and put her arms round him. And that was good.

Della stopped crying and she washed her face. She stood by the window, and looked out at a grey cat on a grey wall in the grey road. Tomorrow was Christmas Day, and she had only one dollar and eighty-seven cents to buy Jim a Christmas present. Her Jim. She wanted very much to buy him something really fine, something to show how much she loved him.

Suddenly, Della turned round and ran over to look in the glass on the wall. Her eyes were bright.

Now, the James Dillingham Youngs had two very special things. One was Jim's gold watch. It once belonged to his father, and, before that, to his grandfather. The other special thing was Della's hair.

Quickly, Della let down her beautiful, long hair. It fell down her back, and it was almost like a coat around her. Then she put her hair up again, quickly. For a second or two she stood still, and cried a little.

Then she put on her old brown coat, and her old brown hat, turned, and left the room. She went downstairs and out into the road, and her eyes were bright.

She walked along by the shops, and stopped when she came to a door with 'Madame Eloise – Hair' on it.

Quickly, Della let down her beautiful, long hair.

Inside there was a fat woman. She did not look like an 'Eloise'.

'Will you buy my hair?' Della asked.

'I buy hair,' Madame replied. 'Take your hat off, then, and show me your hair.'

The beautiful brown hair fell down.

'Twenty dollars,' Madame said, and she touched the hair with her hand.

'Quick! Cut it off! Give me the money!' Della said. The next two hours went quickly. Della was happy because she was looking round the shops for Jim's present.

At last she found it. It was a gold chain for The Watch. Jim loved his watch, but it had no chain. When Della saw this gold chain, she knew immediately that it was right for Jim. She must have it.

The shop took twenty-one dollars from her for it, and she hurried home with the eighty-seven cents.

When she arrived there, she looked at her very short hair in the glass. 'What can I do with it?' she thought. For the next half an hour she was very busy.

Then she looked again in the glass. Her hair was now in very small curls all over her head. 'Oh, dear. I look like a schoolgirl!' she said to herself. 'What's Jim going to say when he sees me?'

At seven o'clock the dinner was nearly ready and

4

'Oh dear,' said Della. 'What's Jim going to say when he sees me?'

Della was waiting. 'Oh, I hope he thinks that I'm still beautiful!' she thought.

The door opened and Jim came in and closed it. He looked very thin and he needed a new coat. His eyes were on Della. She could not understand the look on his face, and she was afraid. He was not angry or surprised. He just watched her, with that strange look on his face.

Della ran to him.

'Jim,' she cried. 'Don't look at me like that. I sold my hair because I wanted to give you a present. It will soon be long again. I had to do it, Jim. Say "Happy Christmas", please. I have a wonderful present for you!'

'You've cut off your hair?' asked Jim.

'Yes. I cut it off and sold it,' Della said. 'But don't you love me any more, Jim? I'm still me.'

Jim looked round the room.

'You say your hair has gone?' he said, almost stupidly.

'Yes. I told you. Because I love you! Shall I get the dinner now, Jim?'

Suddenly Jim put his arms round his Della. Then he took something from his pocket and put it on the table.

'I love you, Della,' he said. 'It doesn't matter if your hair is short or long. But if you open that, you'll see why I was unhappy at first.'

Excited, Della pulled off the paper. Then she gave a little scream of happiness. But a second later there were cries of unhappiness.

Because there were The Combs – the combs for her beautiful hair. When she first saw these combs in the shop window, she wanted them. They were beautiful combs, expensive combs, and now they were her combs. But she no longer had her hair!

6

Della gave a little scream of happiness.

Della picked them up and held them. Her eyes were full of love.

'But my hair will soon be long again, Jim.'

And then Della remembered. She jumped up and cried, 'Oh! Oh!' She ran to get Jim's beautiful present, and she held it out to him.

'Isn't it lovely, Jim? I looked everywhere for it. Now you'll want to look at your watch a hundred times a day. Give it to me! Give me your watch, Jim! Let's see it with its new chain.'

But Jim did not do this. He sat down, put his hands behind his head, and he smiled.

'Della,' he said. 'Let's keep our presents for a time. They're so nice. You see, I sold the watch to get the money to buy your combs. And now, let's have dinner.'

And this was the story of two young people who were very much in love.

Soapy's Choice

Soapy sat on a seat in Madison Square, New York, and looked up at the sky. A dead leaf fell onto his arm. Winter was coming, and Soapy knew that he must make his plans. He moved unhappily on his seat.

He wanted three months in a nice, warm prison, with food and good friends. This was how he usually spent his winters. And now it was time, because, at night on his seat in the square, three newspapers did not keep out the cold.

So Soapy decided to go to prison, and at once began to try his first plan. It was usually easy. He ate dinner in an expensive restaurant. Then he told them he had no money and they called a policeman. Nice and easy, with no trouble.

So Soapy left his seat, and walked slowly along the street. Soon he came to a bright restaurant on Broadway. Ah! This was all right. He just had to get to a table in the restaurant and sit down. That was all, because, when he sat down, people could only see his coat and his shirt, which were not very old. Nobody could see his trousers. He thought about the meal – not too expensive, but good.

But when Soapy went into the restaurant, the waiter saw Soapy's dirty old trousers and terrible shoes.

Strong hands turned him round and helped him out into the street again.

So now he had to think of something different. Soapy walked away from Broadway and soon he found himself on Sixth Avenue. He stopped in front of a shop window and looked at it. It was nice and bright, and everybody in the street could see him. Slowly and carefully he picked up a stone and threw it at the window. The glass broke with a loud noise. People ran round the corner and Soapy was happy, because the man in front was a policeman. Soapy did not move. He stood there with his hands in his pockets, and he smiled. 'I'll soon be in prison now,' he thought.

The policeman came up to Soapy. 'Who did that?' he asked.

'Perhaps I did,' Soapy replied.

But the policeman knew that people who break windows do not stop to talk to policemen. They run away. And just then the policeman saw another man, who was running to catch a bus. So the policeman ran after him. Soapy watched for a minute. Then he walked away. No luck again! He began to feel cross.

*Strong hands turned Soapy round and helped him out
into the street again.*

But on the opposite side of the road he saw a little
restaurant. 'Ah, that'll be all right,' he thought, and he
went in. This time nobody looked at his trousers and
his shoes. He enjoyed his meal, and then he looked up
at the waiter, smiled and said, 'I haven't got any

11

money, you know. Now, call the police. And do it quickly. I'm tired!'

'No police for you!' the waiter answered. 'Hey! Jo!'

Another waiter came, and together they threw Soapy out into the cold street. Soapy lay there, very angry. With difficulty, he stood up. His nice warm prison was still far away, and Soapy was very unhappy. He felt worse because a policeman, who was standing near, laughed and walked away.

Soapy moved on, but he walked for a long time before he tried again. This time it looked easy.

A nice young woman was standing in front of a shop window. Not very far away there was also a police-man. Soapy moved nearer to the young woman. He saw that the policeman was watching him. Then he said to the young woman, with a smile, 'Why don't you come with me, my dear? I can give you a good time.'

The young woman moved away a little and looked more carefully into the shop window. Soapy looked at the policeman. Yes, he was still watching. Then he spoke to the young woman again. In a minute she would call the policeman. Soapy could almost see the prison doors. Suddenly, the young woman took hold of his arm.

'OK,' she said happily. 'If you buy me a drink. Let's

go before that policeman sees us.'

And poor Soapy walked away with the young woman, who still held on to his arm. He was very unhappy.

At the next corner he ran away from the woman. Suddenly he was afraid. 'I'm never going to get to prison,' he thought.

Slowly, he walked on and came to a street with a lot of theatres. There were a lot of people there, rich people in their best clothes. Soapy had to do something to get to prison. He did not want to spend another night on his seat in Madison Square. What could he do? Then he saw a policeman near him, so he began to sing and shout and make a lot of noise. This time they must send him to prison. But the policeman turned his back to Soapy and said to a man who was standing near, 'He's had too much to drink, but he's not dangerous. We'll leave him alone tonight.'

What was the matter with the police? Soapy was really unhappy now, but he stopped making a noise. How could he get to prison? The wind was cold, and he pulled his thin coat around him.

But, just then, inside a shop, he saw a man with an expensive umbrella. The man put his umbrella down near the door, and took out a cigarette. Soapy went into the shop, picked up the umbrella, and, slowly, he

'We'll leave him alone tonight,' said the policeman.

began to walk away. The man came quickly after him.
'That's my umbrella,' he said.

'Oh, is it?' Soapy replied. 'Then why don't you call a
policeman? I took it, and you say it's your umbrella.
Go on, then. Call a policeman! Look! There's one on
the corner.'

The umbrella man looked unhappy. 'Well, you
know, perhaps I've made a mistake. I took it from a
restaurant this morning. If it's yours, well, I'm very
sorry . . .'

14

'Of course it's my umbrella,' Soapy said.

The policeman looked at them – and the umbrella man walked away. The policeman went to help a beautiful young girl to cross the road.

Soapy was really angry now. He threw the umbrella away and said many bad things about policemen. Just because he wanted to go to prison, they did not want to send him there. He could do nothing wrong!

He began to walk back to Madison Square and home – his seat.

But on a quiet corner, Soapy suddenly stopped. Here, in the middle of the city, was a beautiful old church. Through one purple window he could see a soft light, and sweet music was coming from inside the church. The moon was high in the sky and everything was quiet. For a few seconds it was like a country church and Soapy remembered other, happier days. He thought of the days when he had a mother, and friends, and beautiful things in his life.

Then he thought about his life now – the empty days, the dead plans. And then a wonderful thing happened. Soapy decided to change his life and be a new man. 'Tomorrow,' he said to himself, 'I'll go into town and find work. My life will be good again. I'll be somebody important. Everything will be different. I'll . . .'

Soapy felt a hand on his arm. He jumped and looked

For a few seconds Soapy remembered other, happier days.

round quickly – into the face of a policeman!

'What are you doing here?' asked the policeman.

'Nothing,' Soapy answered.

'Then come with me,' the policeman said.

'Three months in prison,' they told Soapy the next day.

16

A Walk in Amnesia

That morning my wife and I said our usual goodbyes. She left her second cup of tea, and she followed me to the front door. She did this every day. She took from my coat a hair which was not there, and she told me to be careful. She always did this. I closed the door, and she went back to her tea.

I am a lawyer and I work very hard. My friend, Doctor Volney, told me not to work so hard. 'You'll be ill,' he said. 'A lot of people who work too hard get very tired, and suddenly they forget who they are. They can't remember anything. It's called amnesia. You need a change and a rest.'

'But I *do* rest,' I replied. 'On Thursday nights my wife and I play a game of cards, and on Sundays she reads me her weekly letter from her mother.'

That morning, when I was walking to work, I thought about Doctor Volney's words. I was feeling very well, and pleased with life.

When I woke up, I was on a train and feeling very

uncomfortable after a long sleep. I sat back in my seat and I tried to think. After a long time, I said to myself, 'I must have a name!' I looked in my pockets. No letter. No papers. Nothing with my name on. But I found three thousand dollars. 'I must be someone,' I thought.

The train was crowded with men who were all very friendly. One of them came and sat next to me. 'Hi! My name's R.P. Bolder – Bolder and Son, from Missouri. You're going to the meeting in New York, of course? What's your name?'

I had to reply to him, so I said quickly, 'Edward Pinkhammer from Cornopolis, Kansas.'

He was reading a newspaper, but every few minutes he looked up from it, to talk to me. I understood from his conversation that he was a druggist, and he thought that I was a druggist, too.

'Are all these men druggists?' I asked.

'Yes, they are,' he answered. 'Like us, they're all going to the yearly meeting in New York.'

After a time, he held out his newspaper to me. 'Look at that,' he said. 'Here's another of those men who run away and then say that they have forgotten who they are. A man gets tired of his business and his family, and he wants to have a good time. He goes away somewhere and when they find him, he says that he

I found three thousand dollars in my pocket.

doesn't know who he is, and that he can't remember anything.'

I took the paper and read this:

Denver, June 12th

Elwyn C. Bellford, an important lawyer in the town, left home three days ago and has not come back. Just before he left, he took out a lot of money from his bank. Nobody has seen him since that day. He is a quiet man who enjoys his work and is happily married. But Mr Bellford works very hard, and it is possible that he has amnesia.

19

'But sometimes people do forget who they are, Mr Bolder,' I said.

'Oh, come on!' Mr Bolder answered. 'It's not true, you know! These men just want something more exciting in their lives – another woman, perhaps. Something different.'

We arrived in New York at about ten o'clock at night. I took a taxi to a hotel, and I wrote the name, 'Edward Pinkhammer', in the hotel book. Suddenly I felt wild and happy – I was free. A man without a name can do anything.

The young man behind the desk at the hotel looked at me a little strangely. I had no suitcase.

'I'm here for the Druggists' Meeting,' I said. 'My suitcase is lost.' I took out some money and gave it to him.

The next day I bought a suitcase and some clothes and I began to live the life of Edward Pinkhammer. I didn't try to remember who or what I was.

The next few days in Manhattan were wonderful – the theatres, the gardens, the music, the restaurants, the night life, the beautiful girls. And during this time I learned something very important – if you want to be happy, you must be free.

Sometimes I went to quiet, expensive restaurants with soft music. Sometimes I went on the river in boats

The next few days in Manhattan were wonderful.

full of noisy young men and their girlfriends. And then there was Broadway, with its theatres and bright lights.

One afternoon I was going back into my hotel when a fat man came and stood in front of me.

'Hello, Bellford!' he cried loudly. 'What are you doing in New York? Is Mrs B. with you?'

'I'm sorry, but you're making a mistake, sir,' I said coldly. 'My name is Pinkhammer. Please excuse me.'

The man moved away, in surprise, and I walked over to the desk. Behind me, the man said something about a telephone.

'Give me my bill,' I said to the man behind the desk,

21

'and bring down my suitcase in half an hour.'

That afternoon I moved to a quiet little hotel on Fifth Avenue.

One afternoon, in one of my favourite restaurants on Broadway, I was going to my table when somebody pulled my arm.

'Mr Bellford,' a sweet voice cried.

I turned quickly and saw a woman who was sitting alone. She was about thirty and she had very beautiful eyes.

'How can you walk past me like that?' she said. 'Didn't you know me?'

I sat down at her table. Her hair was a beautiful red-gold colour.

'Are you sure you know me?' I asked.

'No.' She smiled. 'I never really knew you.'

'Well, my name is Edward Pinkhammer,' I said, 'and I'm from Kansas.'

'So, you haven't brought Mrs Bellford with you, then,' she said, and she laughed. 'You haven't changed much in fifteen years, Elwyn.'

Her wonderful eyes looked carefully at my face.

'No,' she said quietly, 'you haven't forgotten. I told you that you could never forget.'

'I'm sorry,' I answered, 'but that's the trouble. I *have* forgotten. I've forgotten everything.'

22

'You haven't changed much in fifteen years, Elwyn,'
she said.

She laughed. 'Did you know that I married six months after you did? It was in all the newspapers.' She was silent for a minute. Then she looked up at me again. 'Tell me one thing, Elwyn,' she said softly. 'Since that night fifteen years ago, can you touch, smell, or look at white roses – and not think of me?'

'I can only say that I don't remember any of this,' I said carefully. 'I'm very sorry.' I tried to look away from her.

23

She smiled and stood up to leave. Then she held out her hand to me, and I took it for a second. 'Oh yes, you remember,' she said, with a sweet, unhappy smile.

'Goodbye, Elwyn Bellford.'

That night I went to the theatre and when I returned to my hotel, a quiet man in dark clothes was waiting for me.

'Mr Pinkhammer,' he said, 'can I speak with you for a minute? There's a room here.'

I followed him into a small room. A man and a woman were there. The woman was still beautiful, but her face was unhappy and tired. I liked everything about her. The man, who was about forty, came to meet me.

'Bellford,' he said, 'I'm happy to see you again. I told you that you were working too hard. Now you can come home with us. You'll soon be all right.'

'My name', I said, 'is Edward Pinkhammer. I've never seen you before in my life.'

The woman cried out, 'Oh, Elwyn! Elwyn! I'm your wife!' She put her arms round me, but I pushed them away.

'Oh, Doctor Volney! What is the matter with him?' the woman cried.

'Go to your room,' the doctor said to her. 'He'll soon be well again.'

The woman cried out, 'Oh, Elwyn! Elwyn! I'm your wife!'

The woman left, and so did the man in the dark clothes. The man who was a doctor turned to me and said quietly, 'Listen. Your name is not Edward Pinkhammer.'

'I know that,' I replied, 'but a man must have a name. Why not Pinkhammer?'

'Your name', the doctor said, 'is Elwyn Bellford. You are one of the best lawyers in Denver – and that woman is your wife.'

'She's a very fine woman,' I said, after a minute. 'I love the colour of her hair.'

'She's a very good wife,' the doctor replied. 'When you left two weeks ago, she was very unhappy. Then we had a telephone call from a man who saw you in a hotel here.'

'I think I remember him,' I said. 'He called me "Bellford". Excuse me, but who are you?'

'I'm Bobby Volney. I've been your friend for twenty years, and your doctor for fifteen years. Elwyn, try to remember.'

'You say you're a doctor,' I said. 'How can I get better? Does amnesia go slowly or suddenly?'

'Sometimes slowly. Sometimes suddenly.'

'Will you help me, Doctor Volney?' I asked.

'Old friend,' he said, 'I'll do everything possible.'

'Very well. And if you're my doctor, you can't tell anybody what I say.'

'Of course not,' Doctor Volney answered.

I stood up. There were some white roses on the table. I went over to the table, picked up the roses and threw them far out of the window. Then I sat down again.

'I think it will be best, Bobby,' I said, 'to get better suddenly. I'm a little tired of it all now. Go and bring my wife Marian in now. But, oh, Doctor,' I said with a happy smile. 'Oh, my good old friend – it was wonderful!'

Tildy's Moment

Bogle's Family Restaurant on Eighth Avenue is not a famous place, but if you need a large cheap meal, then Bogle's is the place for you. There are twelve tables in the room, six on each side. Bogle himself sits at the desk by the door and takes the money. There are also two waitresses and a Voice. The Voice comes from the kitchen.

At the time of my story, one of the waitresses was called Aileen. She was tall, beautiful and full of life. The name of the other waitress was Tildy. She was small, fat and was not beautiful.

Most of the people who came to eat at Bogle's were men, and they loved the beautiful Aileen. They were happy to wait a long time for their meals because they could look at her. Aileen knew how to hold a conversation with twelve people and work hard at the same time. And all the men wanted to take Aileen dancing or give her presents. One gave her a gold ring and one gave her a little dog.

And poor Tildy?

*In the busy, noisy restaurant men's eyes did not
follow Tildy.*

In the busy, noisy restaurant men's eyes did not follow Tildy. Nobody laughed and talked with her. Nobody asked her to go dancing, and nobody gave her presents. She was a good waitress, but when she stood by the tables, the men looked round her to see Aileen.

But Tildy was happy to work with no thanks, she was happy to see the men with Aileen, she was happy to know that the men loved Aileen. She was Aileen's friend. But deep inside, she, too, wanted a man to love her.

Tildy listened to all Aileen's stories. One day Aileen came in with a black eye. A man hit her because she did not want to kiss him. 'How wonderful to have a black eye for love!' Tildy thought.

One of the men who came to Bogle's was a young man called Mr Seeders. He was a small, thin man, and he worked in an office. He knew that Aileen was not interested in him, so he sat at one of Tildy's tables, said nothing, and ate his fish.

One day when Mr Seeders came in for his meal, he drank too much beer. He finished his fish, got up, put his arm round Tildy, kissed her loudly, and walked out of the restaurant.

For a few seconds Tildy just stood there. Then Aileen said to her, 'Why, Tildy! You bad girl! I must watch you. I don't want to lose my men to you!'

Suddenly Tildy's world changed. She understood now that men could like her and want her as much as Aileen. She, Tildy, could have a love-life, too. Her eyes were bright, and her face was pink. She wanted to tell everybody her secret. When the restaurant was quiet, she went and stood by Bogle's desk.

'Do you know what a man in the restaurant did to me today?' she said. 'He put his arm round me and he kissed me!'

Mr Seeders put his arm round Tildy, and kissed her loudly.

'Really!' Bogle answered. This was good for business. 'Next week you'll get a dollar a week more.'

And when, in the evening, the restaurant was busy again, Tildy put down the food on the tables and said quietly, 'Do you know what a man in the restaurant did to me today? He put his arm round me and kissed me!'

Some of the men in the restaurant were surprised; some of them said, 'Well done!' Men began to smile and say nice things to her. Tildy was very happy. Love was now possible in her grey life.

For two days Mr Seeders did not come again, and in that time Tildy was a different woman. She wore bright clothes, did her hair differently, and she looked taller and thinner. Now she was a real woman because someone loved her. She felt excited, and a little afraid. What would Mr Seeders do the next time he came in?

At four o'clock in the afternoon of the third day, Mr Seeders came in. There were no people at the tables, and Aileen and Tildy were working at the back of the restaurant. Mr Seeders walked up to them.

Tildy looked at him, and she could not speak. Mr Seeders' face was very red, and he looked uncomfortable.

'Miss Tildy,' he said, 'I want to say that I'm sorry for what I did to you a few days ago. It was the drink, you

see. I didn't know what I was doing. I'm very sorry.'
And Mr Seeders left.

But Tildy ran into the kitchen, and she began to cry.
She could not stop crying. She was no longer beautiful.
No man loved her. No man wanted her. The kiss
meant nothing to Mr Seeders. Tildy did not like him
very much, but the kiss was important to her – and
now there was nothing.

But she still had her friend, and Aileen put her arm
round Tildy. Aileen did not really understand, but she
said, 'Don't be unhappy, Tildy. That little Seeders has
got a face like a dead potato! He's nothing. A *real* man
never says sorry!'

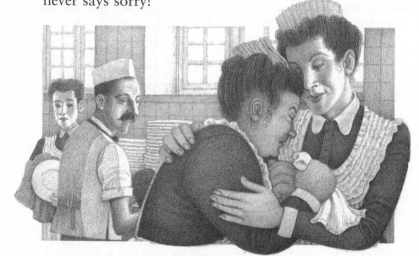

But she still had her friend, and Aileen put her arm
round Tildy.

The Memento

The window of Miss D'Armande's room looked out onto Broadway and its theatres. But Lynette D'Armande turned her chair round and sat with her back to Broadway. She was an actress, and needed the Broadway theatres, but Broadway did not need her.

She was staying in the Hotel Thalia. Actors go there to rest for the summer and then try to get work for the autumn when the little theatres open again. Miss D'Armande's room in this hotel was a small one, but in it there were many mementoes of her days in the theatre, and there were also pictures of some of her best friends. She looked at one of these pictures now, and smiled at it.

'I'd like to know where Lee is now,' she said to herself.

She was looking at a picture of Miss Rosalie Ray, a very beautiful young woman. In the picture, Miss Ray was wearing a very short skirt and she was sitting on a swing. Every night in the theatre she went high in the air on her swing, over the heads of all the people.

When she did this, all the men in the theatre got very excited and stood up. This was because, when her long beautiful legs were high in the air, her yellow garter flew off and fell down to the men below. She did this every evening, and every evening a hundred hands went up to catch the garter. She did other things. She sang, she danced, but when she got onto her swing, all the men stood up. Miss Ray did not have to try very hard to find work in the theatre.

After two years of this, Miss D'Armande remembered, Miss Ray suddenly left the theatre and went to live in the country.

And seventeen minutes after Miss D'Armande said, 'I'd like to know where Lee is now', somebody knocked on the door.

It was, of course, Rosalie Ray.

'Come in,' Miss D'Armande called, and Miss Ray came in. Yes, it was Rosalie. She took off her hat, and Miss D'Armande could see that she looked very tired and unhappy.

'I've got the room above you,' Rosalie said. 'They told me at the desk downstairs that you were here.'

'I've been here since the end of April,' Lynnette replied. 'I begin work again next week, out in a small town. But you left the theatre three months ago, Lee. Why are you here?'

*Rosalie Ray did this every evening, and every evening a
hundred hands went up to catch the garter.*

'I'll tell you, Lynn, but give me a drink first.' Miss D'Armande passed a bottle to her friend.

'Ah, that's good!' said Rosalie. 'My first drink for three months. Yes, Lynn, I left the theatre because I was tired of the life, and because I was tired of men – well, the men who come to the theatre. You know we have to fight them off all the time. They're animals! They ask you to go out with them, they buy you a drink or two – and then they think that they can do what they want! It's terrible! And we work hard, we get very little money for it, we wait to get to the top – and it never happens. But most of all, I left because of the men.

'Well, I saved two hundred dollars and when summer came, I left the theatre and went to a little village by the sea on Long Island. I planned to stay there for the summer, and then learn how to be a better actress.

'But there was another person who was staying in the same house – the Reverend Arthur Lyle. Yes, Lynn, a man of the church! When I saw him for the first time, I fell in love with him at once. He was a fine man and he had a wonderful voice!

'Well, it's only a short story, Lynn. A month later we decided to marry. We planned to live in a little house near the church, with lots of flowers and animals.

'No, I didn't tell him that I was an actress. I wanted to forget it and to put that life behind me.

'Oh, I was happy! I went to church, I helped the women in the village. Arthur and I went for long walks – and that little village was the best place in the world. I wanted to live there for ever . . .

'But one morning, the old woman who worked in the house began to talk about Arthur. She thought that he was wonderful, too. But then she told me that Arthur was in love once before, and that it ended unhappily. She said that, in his desk, he kept a

'Yes, Lynn, I left the theatre because I was tired of men.'

37

memento – something which belonged to the girl. Sometimes he took it out and looked at it. But she didn't know what it was – and his desk was locked.

'That afternoon I asked him about it.

' "Ida," he said, (of course, I used my real name there) "it was before I knew you, and I never met her. It was different from my love for you."

' "Was she beautiful?" I asked.

' "She was very beautiful," replied Arthur.

' "Did you see her often?"

' "About ten times," he said.

' "And this memento – did she send it to you?"

' "It came to me from her," he said.

' "Why did you never meet her?" I asked.

' "She was far above me," he answered. "But, Ida, it's finished. You're not angry, are you?"

' "Why, no. I love you ten times more than before." And I did, Lynn. Can you understand that? What a beautiful love that was! He never met her, never spoke to her, but he loved her, and wanted nothing from her. He was different from other men, I thought – a really good man!

'About four o'clock that afternoon, Arthur had to go out. The door of his room was open, his desk was unlocked, and I decided to look at this memento. I opened the desk and slowly I took out the box and opened it.

'I took one look at that memento, and then I went to my room and packed my suitcase. My wonderful Arthur, this really good man, was no different from all the other men!'

'But, Lee, what was in the box?' Miss D'Armande asked.

'It was one of my yellow garters!' cried Miss Ray.

'Arthur was different from other men, I thought –
a really good man.'

GLOSSARY

actor/actress   a man/woman who works in a theatre, and acts, sings or dances

amnesia   forgetting everything; not knowing your name, your family, where you live, etc.

beer   a drink with alcohol in it

cards (playing cards)   a set of 52 cards used to play games

chain *(n)*   a lot of very small metal rings joined together

choice   something that you choose or decide

comb *(n)*   a piece of metal or wood with long 'teeth' which women use to put up their long hair

curl *(n)*   a little ring of hair

druggist   American word for a person who makes and sells medicines

fall in love with   to begin to love somebody very much

garter   something worn by women round the top of the leg (not usually seen because it is under the skirt)

kiss *(v & n)*   to put your mouth on the mouth of another person to show love

lawyer   a person who has studied the law and who helps people or talks for them in a court of law

lovely   very nice; beautiful

memento   something which helps you to remember somebody

moment   a very short time

pick up   to take something in the hand

Reverend   a name given to a man of the church

rose *(n)*   a summer flower with a sweet smell

sir   a polite word to say to a man when you don't know his name

swing *(n)* a seat on the end of two long ropes, which moves backwards and forwards through the air

throw (past tense **threw**) to move your arm quickly to send something through the air

umbrella a cover on a stick that you hold over you to keep the rain off

waiter/waitress a man/woman who works in a restaurant and brings food to the table

Before Reading

1 Read the introduction on the first page of the book, and the back cover. Are these sentences true? Tick one box for each sentence.

	YES	NO
1 These stories are about famous people.	☐	☐
2 These stories are about people in New York.	☐	☐
3 New York today is very different from the New York in these stories.	☐	☐
4 The people in these stories have unusual jobs and strange lives.	☐	☐

2 Here are the five story titles, with a character from each story. Which of the five things below belongs to each story? Can you guess?

a secret in a desk / too much drink / a gold watch / a prison / a train ride

The Christmas Presents	a housewife	_____
Soapy's Choice	a tramp	_____
A Walk in Amnesia	a lawyer	_____
Tildy's Moment	a waitress	_____
The Memento	an actress	_____

While Reading

Read *The Christmas Presents*. Choose the best question-word for each question, and then answer them.

Why / What

1 . . . did Della cry?
2 . . . two special things did Jim and Della have?
3 . . . did Della sell to Madame Eloise?
4 . . . did Jim buy for Della?
5 . . . couldn't Jim use his present?
6 . . . couldn't Della use her present?

Read *Soapy's Choice*. Are these sentences true (T) or false (F)? Rewrite the false ones with the correct information.

1 Soapy went into an expensive restaurant, but he didn't get a meal.
2 When Soapy broke a window, the policeman ran after him.
3 In the second restaurant, Soapy had a good meal.
4 The young woman called a policeman when Soapy spoke to her.
5 Soapy took a man's umbrella, and then gave it back.
6 In the church, Soapy decided to change his life.
7 The next day, Soapy got a job for three months.

Read *A Walk in Amnesia*. Who said this – Elwyn Bellford or Edward Pinkhammer – and who was he talking to?

1 'But I *do* rest.'
2 'Sometimes people do forget who they are.'
3 'Are you sure you know me?'
4 'I've never seen you before in my life.'
5 'How can I get better?'
6 'I'm a little tired of it all now.'
7 'It was wonderful!'

Read *Tildy's Moment*, and then answer the questions.

1 What was Tildy like?
2 Why did all the men in Bogle's like to watch Aileen?
3 Why did Mr Seeders kiss Tildy?
4 How was Tildy different after the kiss?
5 What did Mr Seeders do the next time he came in?
6 Why did Tildy begin to cry?

Read *The Memento*. Here are some untrue sentences about this story. Change them into true sentences.

1 Miss Ray left the theatre because she was afraid of men.
2 Arthur knew that Ida was the actress Rosalie Ray.
3 Arthur kept a letter from his first love in his desk.
4 Arthur never saw Miss Ray in the theatre.
5 Miss Ray left Arthur because he was not like other men.

After Reading

1 In *The Christmas Presents*, perhaps Jim thought about his present for Della on his way home from work. Complete the text with these words. (Use one word in each gap.)

beautiful, because, belonged, chain, combs, do, door, face, feeling, fine, grey, home, important, long, love, must, no, opens, present, sell, use, when, without

Well, it's a cold, _____ night again, but I'm _____ great. I'm going _____ to Della, and I've got a wonderful Christmas _____ for her. I didn't want to _____ my gold watch, _____ it was so special to me. I was only eighteen _____ my father gave it to me, and before that it _____ to my grandfather. But what could I _____? I had _____ money, and Della _____ have a present – Christmas _____ presents is terrible! I couldn't _____ the watch very often because I don't have a _____ for it. And Della is more _____ than a gold watch – I wanted to buy her something really _____, something to show how much I _____ her. I know she wants these _____, and they'll look _____ in her _____ brown hair. I can't wait to see her _____ when she _____ my present. Ah, here's my front _____ now . . .

2 At the end of *Soapy's Choice*, the policeman asks Soapy questions in the police station. Put their conversation in the correct order and write in the speakers' names. The policeman speaks first (number 6).

1 _____ 'It's a nice story, Soapy, but I don't believe it. Now go and sit over there.'

2 _____ 'Nothing! I was thinking, that's all.'

3 _____ 'Your mother! I don't think so, Soapy. I think you wanted to go into the church and look for money.'

4 _____ 'So what was your plan, Soapy? Drinking and fighting? Taking somebody's coat and selling it?'

5 _____ 'Huh! Policemen! When you're bad, they leave you alone, and when you're good, they take you away!'

6 _____ 'OK, Soapy, what were you doing outside that church?'

7 _____ 'Thinking about what?'

8 _____ 'Look, I know I've done some bad things in the past, but today I've decided to change my life and be a new man. I'm going to find some work and . . .'

9 _____ 'No, that's not true! That wasn't my plan.'

10 _____ 'Well, I heard the music inside the church, and I started to think about my mother, and my friends, and all the happy times . . .'

3 In *A Walk in Amnesia*, Elwyn Bellford returned to Denver, and a few days later had a talk with Dr Volney. Complete their conversation. (Use as many words as you like.)

DR VOLNEY: Now, Elwyn, tell me why you ran away.

ELWYN: Well, suddenly I _____.

DR VOLNEY: But I thought you enjoyed your work?

ELWYN: Yes, I do, but _____.

DR VOLNEY: And tired of Marian too?

ELWYN: No, I still love her, but _____.

DR VOLNEY: So what did you do in New York?

ELWYN: I _____.

DR VOLNEY: And are you planning to be Edward Pinkhammer again some time?

ELWYN: No, I don't think so – but _____!

4 Mr Seeders wrote to a friend about his moment with Tildy. Complete his letter with these linking words. (You will need to use some of them more than once.)

and / because / but / so / then / when / who

Dear Jack,

I did a terrible thing today. I go to Bogle's for lunch, _____ the food is cheap _____ I love watching Aileen, _____ is one of the waitresses. She's tall and beautiful, _____ she's not interested in me, _____ I always sit at Tildy's table. Tildy's a good waitress, _____ she's small and fat.

I don't usually drink at lunch time, _____ today I had two beers. Suddenly I felt strong, and tall, and clever, _____ I went up to Tildy, put my arm round her, _____ gave her a big kiss. _____ I went back to work.

Now I've got a headache, _____ I feel very stupid. What shall I say to Tildy _____ I see her again, Jack? Please help.

Yours truly,

William Seeders

5 In *The Memento*, perhaps Arthur Lyle wrote to Ida after she left, and Ida wrote back to him. Which sentences belong to which letter? Put the pieces of each letter together, and in the right order.

1 My dear Ida, why did you go away so suddenly?

2 Dear Mr Lyle, that 'old yellow garter' was mine,

3 which came from an actress on Broadway.

4 So I won't marry you, and don't write to me again. Ida.

5 but when I saw my garter in your desk,

6 I love you so much – please come back. Arthur.

7 and *I* was that actress on Broadway!

8 It's only an old yellow garter,

9 I knew that you were just like other men.

10 Was it because of that memento?

11 I thought that you were a really good man,

12 She's not important to me, but you are!

6 **Here is a new illustration for one of the stories. Find the best place for it, and answer these questions.**

The picture goes on page _____, in the story _____.

1 Who is the woman in the picture?

2 What has she just found?

3 How does she feel at this moment, and why?

Now write a caption for the illustration.

Caption: _____

7 Here are some new titles for the five stories. Which titles go with which stories? Some are better titles than others. Can you say why?

Rosalie and the Reverend

A Present of Love

Escape to New York

How to Go to Prison

The Unhappy Waitress

A Poor Christmas

A Secret in a Box

Nothing to Give But Love

Take Me to Prison!

Elwyn Runs Away

Little Kiss, Big Mistake

Men are All the Same

A Moment of Change

Remembering White Roses

Kissing the Wrong Girl

8 Here is a new ending for each story. Which do you prefer – the ending in the book or the ending here? Explain why, or write a new ending yourself.

1 Jim finds $20 in the street and buys his watch back. Della sells the combs and buys a new hat.

2 The policeman feels sorry for Soapy, and gives him an easy job at the police station.

3 Two months after Elwyn goes back to Denver, his wife takes all his money and runs away to Paris.

4 Now Tildy knows that men like her, she gets a job as an actress. Soon she is very famous.

5 Rosalie and Arthur forget their past lives and marry.

ABOUT THE AUTHOR

William Sydney Porter (O. Henry) was born in North Carolina, USA, in 1862. When he was twenty, he went to Texas where he worked in different offices and then in a bank. In 1887 he married a young woman called Athol Estes. He and Athol were very happy together, and at this time he began writing short stories. His most famous story is *The Gift of the Magi* (called *The Christmas Presents* in this book), and many people think that Della in this story is based on his wife Athol.

In 1896 Porter ran away to Honduras because people said he stole money from the bank when he was working there in 1894. A year later he came back to Texas to see Athol, who was dying, and in 1898 he was sent to prison. During his time there he published many short stories, using the name 'O. Henry', and when he left prison in 1901, he was already a famous writer. He then lived in New York until his death in 1910.

Porter's stories are both sad and funny, and show a great understanding of the everyday lives of people like shop girls and office workers. He wrote about six hundred stories and made a lot of money, but he was a very unhappy man. When he died, he had only twenty-three cents in his pocket, and his last words were:

'Turn up the lights; I don't want to go home in the dark.'

OXFORD BOOKWORMS LIBRARY

Classics • Crime & Mystery • Factfiles • Fantasy & Horror
Human Interest • Playscripts • Thriller & Adventure
True Stories • World Stories

The OXFORD BOOKWORMS LIBRARY provides enjoyable reading in English, with a wide range of classic and modern fiction, non-fiction, and plays. It includes original and adapted texts in seven carefully graded language stages, which take learners from beginner to advanced level. An overview is given on the next pages.

All Stage 1 titles are available as audio recordings, as well as over eighty other titles from Starter to Stage 6. All Starters and many titles at Stages 1 to 4 are specially recommended for younger learners. Every Bookworm is illustrated, and Starters and Factfiles have full-colour illustrations.

The OXFORD BOOKWORMS LIBRARY also offers extensive support. Each book contains an introduction to the story, notes about the author, a glossary, and activities. Additional resources include tests and worksheets, and answers for these and for the activities in the books. There is advice on running a class library, using audio recordings, and the many ways of using Oxford Bookworms in reading programmes. Resource materials are available on the website <www.oup.com/bookworms>.

The *Oxford Bookworms Collection* is a series for advanced learners. It consists of volumes of short stories by well-known authors, both classic and modern. Texts are not abridged or adapted in any way, but carefully selected to be accessible to the advanced student.

You can find details and a full list of titles in the *Oxford Bookworms Library Catalogue* and *Oxford English Language Teaching Catalogues*, and on the website <www.oup.com/bookworms>.

THE OXFORD BOOKWORMS LIBRARY
GRADING AND SAMPLE EXTRACTS

STARTER • 250 HEADWORDS

present simple – present continuous – imperative –
can/cannot, must – *going to* (future) – simple gerunds ...

Her phone is ringing – but where is it?

Sally gets out of bed and looks in her bag. No phone. She looks under the bed. No phone. Then she looks behind the door. There is her phone. Sally picks up her phone and answers it. *Sally's Phone*

STAGE 1 • 400 HEADWORDS

... past simple – coordination with *and*, *but*, *or* –
subordination with *before*, *after*, *when*, *because*, *so* ...

I knew him in Persia. He was a famous builder and I worked with him there. For a time I was his friend, but not for long. When he came to Paris, I came after him – I wanted to watch him. He was a very clever, very dangerous man. *The Phantom of the Opera*

STAGE 2 • 700 HEADWORDS

... present perfect – *will* (future) – *(don't) have to, must not, could* –
comparison of adjectives – simple *if* clauses – past continuous –
tag questions – *ask/tell* + infinitive ...

While I was writing these words in my diary, I decided what to do. I must try to escape. I shall try to get down the wall outside. The window is high above the ground, but I have to try. I shall take some of the gold with me – if I escape, perhaps it will be helpful later. *Dracula*

54

... should, may – present perfect continuous – *used to* – past perfect –
causative – relative clauses – indirect statements ...

Of course, it was most important that no one should see
Colin, Mary, or Dickon entering the secret garden. So Colin
gave orders to the gardeners that they must all keep away
from that part of the garden in future. ***The Secret Garden***

... past perfect continuous – passive (simple forms) –
would conditional clauses – indirect questions –
relatives with *where/when* – gerunds after prepositions/phrases ...

I was glad. Now Hyde could not show his face to the world
again. If he did, every honest man in London would be proud
to report him to the police. ***Dr Jekyll and Mr Hyde***

... future continuous – future perfect –
passive (modals, continuous forms) –
would have conditional clauses – modals + perfect infinitive ...

If he had spoken Estella's name, I would have hit him. I was so
angry with him, and so depressed about my future, that I could
not eat the breakfast. Instead I went straight to the old house.
Great Expectations

... passive (infinitives, gerunds) – advanced modal meanings –
clauses of concession, condition

When I stepped up to the piano, I was confident. It was as if I
knew that the prodigy side of me really did exist. And when I
started to play, I was so caught up in how lovely I looked that
I didn't worry how I would sound. ***The Joy Luck Club***

BOOKWORMS · HUMAN INTEREST · STAGE 2

Stories from the Five Towns

ARNOLD BENNETT

Retold by Nick Bullard

Arnold Bennett is famous for his stories about the Five Towns and the people who live there. They look and sound just like other people, and, like all of us, sometimes they do some very strange things. There's Sir Jee, who is a rich businessman. So why is he making a plan with a burglar? Then there is Toby Hall. Why does he decide to visit Number 11 Child Row, and who does he find there? And then there are the Hessian brothers and Annie Emery – and the little problem of twelve thousand pounds.

BOOKWORMS · CRIME & MYSTERY · STAGE 2

Sherlock Holmes Short Stories

SIR ARTHUR CONAN DOYLE

Retold by Clare West

Sherlock Holmes is the greatest detective of them all. He sits in his room, and smokes his pipe. He listens, and watches, and thinks. He listens to the steps coming up the stairs; he watches the door opening – and he knows what question the stranger will ask.

In these three of his best stories, Holmes has three visitors to the famous flat in Baker Street – visitors who bring their troubles to the only man in the world who can help them.